JESUS, I COME

Jesus, I Come

DAILY DEVOTIONALS ON PERSONAL REVIVAL FROM THE HYMN, "JESUS, I COME"

Gwendolyn Harmon

Learning Ladyhood Press

Copyright © 2021 by Gwendolyn Harmon

All rights reserved. No part of this book may be reproduced in any manner whatsoever without written permission except in the case of brief quotations embodied in critical articles and reviews.

All Scripture quoted is from the King James Version

First Printing, 2021

To the discouraged Christian:
because I have been one, too.

"Draw nigh to God, and He will draw nigh to you."
James 4:8

Contents

Preface		1
1	Out of my Bondage	5
2	God's Freedom	7
3	Health	9
4	God's Wealth	11
5	Into Thyself	13
6	Failure	15
7	The Gain of the Cross	17
8	Earth's Sorrows	19
9	Calm	21
10	Jubilant Psalm	23
11	Unrest	25
12	God's Blessed Will	27
13	Out of Myself	29
14	Raptures Above	31
15	Upward	33
16	The Fear of the Tomb	35
17	Eternal Joy and Light	37

18	Ruin Untold	39
19	God's Shelter	41
20	Ever Beholding	43
21	Come	45

Preface

Every believer hits a wall at some point. Sometimes we call it a "dry spell:" we do all the things a Christian is supposed to do, and yet we don't feel close to God. We read our Bibles, go to church, and pray, but nothing seems to help. We busy ourselves with serving others; but all the while we have this gnawing guilt that, while we're pretending on the outside that all is as it should be, the truth of our hearts is that it just isn't.

For me, a dry spell usually coincides with some disappointment or circumstance I'm struggling with. I often don't realize just how much I'm struggling right away. I keep myself busy and try to stuff everything inside, until there's just no more room and it all comes flooding out.

I feel far from God and far from other people, locked in a misery I know God doesn't want me stuck in. That's usually when God begins to tug at my heart, calling me to come to Him.

Whether you're in a dry spell, or just need to take a break from your busy life for just a few minutes to draw near to God, I pray that the Holy Spirit will use the truths of these studies to work in your heart, and that you, too, would experience the freedom, light, and joy of His presence.

Jesus, I Come

Out of my bondage, sorrow and night,
Jesus, I come, Jesus, I come;
Into Thy freedom, gladness and light,
Jesus, I come to Thee.
Out of my sickness into Thy health,
Out of my want and into Thy wealth,
Out of my sin and into Thyself,
Jesus, I come to Thee.

~

Out of my shameful failure and loss,
Jesus, I come, Jesus, I come;
Into the glorious gain of Thy cross,
Jesus, I come to Thee.
Out of earth's sorrows, into Thy balm,
Out of life's storms and into Thy calm,
Out of distress to jubilant psalm,
Jesus, I come to Thee.

~

Out of unrest and arrogant pride,
Jesus, I come, Jesus, I come;
Into Thy blessed will to abide,
Jesus, I come to Thee.
Out of myself to well in Thy love,
Out of despair into rapture above,
Upward for aye on wings like a dove,
Jesus, I come to Thee.

~

Out of the fear and dread of the tomb,
Jesus, I come, Jesus, I come;
Into the joy and light of Thy home,
Jesus, I come to Thee.
Out of the depths of ruin untold,
Into the peace of Thy sheltering fold,
Ever Thy glorious face to behold,
Jesus, I come to Thee.

William T. Sleeper

1

Out of my Bondage

Out of my bondage, sorrow, and night
Jesus, I come, Jesus, I come

Bondage, sorrow, and night. That's a good summary of what it's like to be distant from God. But have you ever considered that our distance from God is invariably self-inflicted? Nothing but our own sin can separate us from God, so the very first step to personal revival is to heed the words of John the Baptist: *"Behold, the Lamb of God, which taketh away the sin of the world." (John 1:29)*

Why was Jesus needed to take away the sin of the world? Because *"all have sinned, and come short of the glory of God." (Romans 3:23)* We must recognize that it was *our* sin, yours and mine, that sent Jesus to the cross. It was for you he died. He who was perfect, sinless, and completely holy, took *your* sins --every one of them-- on Himself. The first step for anyone is to ask for the forgiveness which Christ has already bought: to trust that His sacrifice, His death, burial, and resurrection have purchased your pardon from sin and your entrance into heaven. That is salvation.

But being saved doesn't mean we never sin again. That is why we must be careful that nothing comes between us and the Savior. To the drifting church in Ephesus, Jesus said: *"Remember therefore from whence Thou art fallen, and repent and do the first works." (Revelation 2:5)*

To see ourselves as we really are, we must first see Jesus as He is: recognizing just how short we fall in comparison. Consider this description from Hebrews: *"For such a High Priest became us, who is holy, harmless, undefiled, separate from sinners, and made higher than the heavens; who needeth not daily, as those high priests, to offer up sacrifice, first for His own sins, and then for the people's: for this He did once, when He offered up Himself." (7:26)*

Christ offered Himself up, once and for all, so that you could be freed from bondage. The question is: are you living in the freedom of the cross, or are you in bondage to sin? The first step is to see your sin as Christ sees it and then confess it to God.

What sin is keeping you from enjoying God's presence today?

2

God's Freedom

"Into Thy freedom, gladness, and light,
Jesus, I come to Thee"

Seeing our sin as Jesus sees it may be an overwhelming experience. Jesus' death was required as payment even for the "little sins" --the things we tend to excuse or brush off as no big deal. When we realize just how wretchedly we compare with the holy God, it can be easy to feel like we are hopelessly flawed. And we are, apart from Christ.

That is where grace comes in. Ephesians 2:8-9 tells us,

"For by grace are ye saved through faith; and that not of yourselves: it is the gift of God: Not of works, lest any man should boast."

As wonderful as our salvation is, the work of grace does not end there:

"As ye have therefore received Christ Jesus the Lord, so walk ye in Him: Rooted and built up in Him, and stablished in the faith, as ye have been taught, abounding therein with thanksgiving." (Colossians 2:6-7)

The grace God offers for salvation is the same grace He offers for our daily walk of sanctification (the process of growing to be more like the Lord). God wants us to walk in the victory of the cross, not the bondage of sin. We can only do that through the empowering of the Holy Spirit, which is as freely given as salvation: we just have to accept the grace God offers.

Jesus said: *"If ye continue in My word, then are ye my disciples indeed; and ye shall know the truth, and the truth shall make you free." (John 8:31-32)* The truths of God's Word free us. We *can* live each day in triumph, basking in the light of Christ and the victory He has already won on our behalf.

It is all of grace: we have but to yield to God, *"which worketh in you both to will and to do of His good pleasure." (Philippians 2:13)* Whatever sin has imprisoned you, the glorious truth remains that Christ has *already* freed you. Live in the freedom of His victory!

What has Christ offered you grace to conquer today?

3

Health

"Out of my sickness, into Thy health"

Psalm 67:1-2 makes an interesting statement:

"God be merciful unto us, and bless us; and cause His face to shine upon us; Selah. That Thy way may be known upon the earth, Thy saving health among all nations."

When we are close to God in the place of blessing, we become healthier spiritually, emotionally, and even physically. Of course, that does not mean we will never be sick, or that we are somehow impervious to physical maladies. But the fact is, God made us. He designed how our bodies work; and when we live our lives God's way, we live the way our bodies were designed to best function. Proverbs 3 fleshes this out for us:

"Be not wise in thine own eyes: fear the Lord, and depart from evil. It shall be health to thy navel, and marrow to thy bones." (v.5-8)

The word "navel" literally means "twisted," and is used here in reference to the umbilical cord, denoting the humanity's first source of strength. Just as an unborn infant is totally dependent upon the nutrition delivered through the umbilical cord, God's children are all dependent upon Him for strength, both spiritual and physical.

The phrase "marrow to thy bones" means literally just that: bone marrow. The function of bone marrow is to produce blood cells (which keep your body healthy) and to store fat (a source of energy.)

When we do things God's way, we are strengthened, made healthier, and defended against infection. Think about that from a spiritual standpoint: it's a powerful illustration of what our relationship with God does for us.

Proverbs 4:20-21 says, *"My son, attend to my words; incline thine ear unto my sayings. Let them not depart from thine eyes; keep them in the midst of thine heart. For they are life unto those that find them, and health to all their flesh."*

That word "flesh" literally refers to the physical body. Sin affects every part of us: and obedience does, too. The way to physical, mental, emotional, and spiritual health is submission and obedience to God's Word in each of those areas of our lives.

In what area is the Holy Spirit prompting you to be healthier today?

4

God's Wealth

"Out of my want and into Thy wealth"

Surrender to God's will and obedience to His Word affects our health, but it also affects our wealth.

Often, some kind of pressure is necessary to push us out of a rut in our relationship with God. Sometimes, that pressure is financial. I've found that for the Christian, there are usually just two reasons for financial pressure: as a judgement on disobedience or an opportunity to build our faith.

In the book of Haggai, God's people had been neglecting the Lord's house. They had built their own houses, but had not found time or resources to build God's house. Here is what God had to say about their situation:

"Now therefore thus saith the Lord of hosts; Consider your ways. Ye have sown much, and bring in little; ye eat, but ye have not enough; ye drink, but ye are not filled with drink; ye clothe you, but there is none warm; and he that earneth wages earneth wages to put it into a bag with holes." (Haggai 1:5-6)

And again a couple verses later,

"Ye looked for much, and, lo, it came to little; and when ye brought it home, I did blow upon it. Why? Saith the Lord of hosts. Because of Mine house that is waste, and ye run every man unto his own house." (1:9)

God was withholding His hand of provision in order to call their attention to the fact that there was something between them and their God. There was an area of disobedience that needed to be addressed.

But that is not always the reason for financial pressure. God often uses physical needs to give us opportunity to trust Him to provide. And we can trust Him! Philippians 4:19 says,

"But my God shall supply all your need according to His riches in glory by Christ Jesus"

God's provision of our needs comes from His own riches. God's wealth is unlimited, but in His goodness, God only gives us what we need. In God's eyes, wealth is not a measure of spirituality, rather, it is a means He often uses to draw our attention to an area of disobedience or an opportunity to build our faith.

To come to God means to surrender to His will for our wealth, trusting that what He has provided is and always will be enough.

To what is the Holy Spirit calling your attention in your finances today?

5

Into Thyself

"Out of my sin and into Thyself,
Jesus, I come to Thee."

The world likes to tell us to "be ourselves." However, God tells us to be like *Him*. When we come to God, we surrender not only to His view of what our sin is, but also to whom He says we are in Him.

In Christ:

- We are chosen *"in Him before the foundation of the world, that we should be holy and without blame before Him in love." (Ephesians 1:4)*
- We are *"His workmanship, created in Christ Jesus unto good works, which God hath before ordained that we should walk in them." (Ephesians 2:10)*
- We are *"no more strangers and foreigners, but fellowcitizens with the saints, and of the household of God." (Ephesians 2:19)*
- We are justified. *(Romans 5:1)*
- We are adopted, made joint-heirs with Christ. *(Romans 8:15-17)*
- We are free from sin. *(Romans 6:18)*

- We are loved, unconditionally and irrevocably. *(Romans 8:33-39)*
- We are God's temple. *(1 Corinthians 3:16)*
- We are empowered to obey by the very strength of Christ Himself. *(Philippians 4:13)*

These are just a few of the truths found throughout Scripture that tell us what our identity really is. When we come to God, we acknowledge not only who we are as *sinners* saved by grace, but also who we are in Christ as *saved* sinners, having entered into the riches of Christ.

As Ephesians 2:1-7 says, *"And you hath He quickened, who were dead in trespasses and sins; Wherein in time past ye walked according to the course of this world, according to the prince of the power of the air, the spirit that now worketh in the children of disobedience: Among whom also we all had our conversation in times past in the lusts of our flesh, fulfilling the desires of the flesh and of the mind; and were by nature the children of wrath, even as others. But God, who is rich in mercy; for His great love wherewith He loved us, Even when we were dead in sins, hath quickened us together with Christ (by grace are ye saved;) And hath raised us up together, and made us sit together in heavenly places in Christ Jesus: That in the ages to come He might show the exceeding riches of His grace in His kindness toward us through Christ Jesus."*

What aspect of your identity in Christ is the Holy Spirit leading you to embrace today?

6

Failure

"Out of my shameful failure and loss,
Jesus, I come, Jesus, I come"

David was the one whom God Himself called a man after His own heart. He was the one God chose to replace Saul as king of Israel. But he was also a man who failed spectacularly. He took the wife of one of his most faithful mighty men, then tried to cover it up, finally resorting to giving an order that would cause that man to be killed in battle.

Adultery.   Deceit.   Murder.

These are failings indeed. But though David had sinned grievously, God didn't cast him off. He sent the prophet Nathan to tell him a story about a man who killed his neighbor's pet sheep instead of his own to feed his guest. David was furious, and declared that the man should die, and restore the lamb fourfold. Nathan replied with words I'm sure David did not expect to hear:

"Thou art the man." (2 Samuel 12:7)

Did David rage? Did he excuse his actions? Did he order his guards to strike Nathan dead or drag him off to the deepest, darkest dungeon? No, he did what a heart accustomed to fellowship with God does: he repented.

He told Nathan *"I have sinned against the Lord," (2 Sam. 12:13)* and out of his heart flowed Psalm 51.

"Have mercy upon me, O God, according to Thy lovingkindness: according unto the multitude of Thy tender mercies blot out my transgressions. Wash me thoroughly from mine iniquity, and cleanse me from my sin. For I acknowledge my transgressions: my sin is ever before me." (v.1-3)

David's response when confronted with his failure was humility. He didn't try to argue or deny it. He didn't try to defend his pride. He simply agreed with God's estimation of his sin and plead for mercy.

We, too, are called to confess our sins and respond to our failures honestly. 1 John has a precious promise for those who do:

"If we confess our sins, He is faithful and just to forgive us our sins, and to cleanse us from all unrighteousness." (1 John 1:9)

What is the Holy Spirit calling you to confess today?

7

The Gain of the Cross

"Into the glorious gain of Thy cross,
Jesus, I come to Thee."

A proper view of our failures can be staggering; but as we humbly acknowledge our sin before God, our hearts are softened and our pride is broken down. The stony, hard-packed earth of our hearts is transformed into the good soil needed for God's reviving work to take root. It is then that we are able to see the cross as it is: the source of our glorious gain.

In Philippians 3:7-10, Paul states: *"But what things were gain to me, those I counted loss for Christ. Yea doubtless, and I count all things but loss for the excellency of the knowledge of Christ Jesus my Lord: for whom I have suffered the loss of all things, and do count them but dung, that I may win Christ, and be found in Him, not having mine own righteousness, which is of the law, but that which is through the faith of Christ, the righteousness which is of God by faith: that I may know Him, and the power of His resurrection, and the fellowship of His sufferings, being made conformable unto His death."*

What Paul is saying here is that the very things he had been proud of before salvation, he now counted as worthless, even vile. When he chose to follow Christ, Paul lost his status, (and likely some wealth that went along with it,) many of his friends, his reputation, everything that made him who he was. But did he grumble about those things left behind? Did he wallow in misery, paralyzed by guilt for having persecuted the Christians in Jerusalem? No. We see him focusing on what matters: the excellency of the knowledge of Christ Jesus.

He left it all behind: the shame of his now-forgiven past, the things he had lost. He left it all in the dust and fixed his eyes on the gain of the cross: *"the righteousness of God by faith."*

What does God want you to *"count as loss"* today, focusing instead on what He has given you?

8

Earth's Sorrows

"Out of earth's sorrows into Thy balm,"

This world is full of sorrows. Just a quick look at the news can be enough to throw us into despondency and despair. We look around and find that sorrow surrounds us: sorrow over the state of our nation, sorrow over the persecution of Christians around the world, sorrow over a health diagnosis, sorrow over the loss of a loved one, sorrow over a lost and dying world, sorrow over broken relationships, sorrow over shattered dreams. No matter where we look in this world, we find something to be sorrowful about.

And then the world calls to us: "do more of what makes you happy." It sounds like a good idea at first, but when we look around, it becomes clear that this particular philosophy only leads us into more sin, and sin only ever results in sorrow. This world has no lasting happiness to offer, however loudly it calls to the contrary.

But then, there's God, who says to us, *"These things have I spoken unto you, that My joy might remain in you, and that your joy might be full." (John 15:11)* God never intended for His children to live in sorrow. That came upon us because of Adam and Eve's choice to sin. *(Genesis 3)* And we, too, have chosen to sin, bringing even more sorrow upon ourselves. We are broken people living in a broken world, but God offers to make us whole. He wants us to have joy, and He wants that joy to be *full*.

So, what are the "these things" Jesus spoke to us so that we might have joy? The first ten verses in John 15 are all about abiding in Christ, and letting His love abide in us. The way to joy is to get close to God and to depend on Him alone for our comfort and satisfaction, for He is the *"God of all comfort" (2 Corinthians 1:3)*

What sorrows does God want you to seek His comfort for today?

9

Calm

"Out of life's storms and into Thy calm"

When I was little, I used to enjoy storms. That is, I enjoyed them up to a point. As long as I felt safe, the rain and wind, thunder and lightning felt like an adventure. But if it got *too* stormy, the adventure turned to a nightmare.

When my family moved a few years ago to a house surrounded by trees, the smallest windstorm suddenly became terrifying, because I now realized that there was a possibility some of those trees could topple over on our house and crush us. Once the heart is convinced of impending danger, the flood of fear can be overwhelming.

In Matthew 14, Jesus' disciples faced the terror of a storm. They were toiling busily, trying to keep their ship afloat, when they saw something that terrified them more than the storm. It was what looked like a man walking on top of the waves. Immediately, they cried out in fear, thinking it must be a ghost, but it was Jesus. He told them, *"Be of good cheer; it is I; be not afraid." (v. 27)*

That was when Peter made his bold request: *"Lord, if it be Thou, bid me come unto Thee on the water." (v.28)* Jesus told him to come, and out he stepped. There he was, in the middle of a storm, walking *on* the water towards Jesus. I have often wondered how he must have felt in that first moment when his foot hit the water and found a firm footing. The ship was still tossing, the waves were still rolling, the wind was still boisterous, but in that moment, Peter was calm. Why? Because when he stepped out of that boat, he stepped into the calm of Jesus.

Jesus did not fear the storm, because He *made* it. He had created the wind, waves, and the rain in the first place. Jesus had no reason to be afraid, therefore Peter had no reason to be afraid. But it was not long before Peter took his eyes off Jesus and looked at the storm. He immediately began to sink and cried out for help. Jesus took his hand and lifted him up, saying, *"O thou of little faith, wherefore didst thou doubt?" (v.31)*

Our lives can be stormy at times, and if we're not careful, we can sink into the waves of panic and become paralyzed with fear. But when we choose to walk with Jesus, our feet find firm footing in the peace and certainty of knowing that He is in control. His love for us is perfect, and *that* casts out all our fear. (I John 4:18)

What storm have you faced recently? Did you walk or sink?

10

Jubilant Psalm

"Out of distress to jubilant psalm,
Jesus, I come to Thee."

It was midnight. Paul and Silas had been falsely accused, arrested, then beaten before the magistrates. After their skin had been lacerated by the gruesome flogging of *"many stripes,"* (Acts 16:23) the two men were thrown into the inner prison, where the jailer fastened their feet to what the Bible refers to as *"stocks."* With their feet thus immobilized, it seems that the injured men had only two options: sit up all night or lay back on the hard ground. There was no way to ease the pain of their wounds, and no way to get any rest. There had been no trial, and no indication of what would be done to them when the morning dawned. It was a distressing situation, indeed.

Imagine, then, echoing through the walls of that dark, dirty prison in the middle of the night, two voices, raised in song. It was not a song of distress or lament, but a song of praise! Paul and Silas, feet still bound in stocks, backs still raw, still painful, and likely still bleeding, were praying and singing praises to God. In Acts 5, we see a similar reaction, where the apostles were threatened and beaten, and went away rejoicing. Why? The Bible says that they were *"rejoicing that they were counted worthy to suffer shame for His name." (Acts 5:41)*

The distress of the situation, the pain of their wounds; they saw it all as nothing compared to the glory of being used by God to further His kingdom. Paul and Silas saw the fruit of their sufferings when God sent an earthquake and the jailor came to them asking, "Sirs, what must I do to be saved?"

The suffering God had allowed was for a purpose. Whatever distress you may be facing, God means that for a purpose as well. Isaiah 61:3 speaks of some things Christ would do for His people:

"To give them beauty for ashes, the oil of joy for mourning, the garment of praise for the spirit of heaviness; that they might be called trees of righteousness, the planting of the Lord, that He might be glorified."

God desires us to face distressing circumstances with the joy of knowing He is with us, both to comfort and to enable us to do exactly what He desires us to do in the situation. He wants us to let go of our longing to control, our tight grip on the way *we* want things to be, and to praise Him for what He plans to do with the circumstances He has allowed.

What distress does God want you to turn into praise of Him today?

11

Unrest

"Out of unrest and arrogant pride,
Jesus, I come, Jesus, I come"

Jonah was sitting under a cobbled together shelter, stewing. After all, he had plenty to complain about. He'd been in a storm so fierce the sailors thought the ship would sink, he was thrown overboard and swallowed by a great fish, then spat up on land. He had proclaimed God's message of certain doom on his nation's worst enemies, but now, instead of watching them experience the judgement they so richly deserved, he was sitting in the hot sun watching absolutely nothing happen.

Just as he feared would happen, the Ninevites had repented, and God had withdrawn His hand of judgement in a wholly unmerited display of mercy. Imagine! For such cruel and wicked people as the inhabitants of Nineveh!

As Jonah sat, God caused a gourd plant to grow up and furnish the shade Jonah's improvised booth had not succeeded in providing. Jonah was *"exceeding glad of the gourd"*. *(Jonah 4:6)* But then, God sent a worm to eat the plant, and Jonah again begins to fuss at God again. How dare God take away his shade!

If ever there were a picture of unrest and arrogant pride, Jonah would have been it. In that moment, upset with God for sparing a whole city full of people, upset with God for *not* sparing one single plant, upset with God for not doing things the way *he* thought they should have been done, Jonah was blind to his own sin while fuming over the sins of others.

The storm, the fish, the unceremonious spewing of Jonah onto the shore; all of it was directly due to his own refusal to do the one thing that God had asked of him. Jonah was a prophet of the Most High God, and yet he was unwilling to deliver God's call to repentance to the very people who had demonstrated such deep need of His mercy. Jonah was unwilling to go, unwilling to forgive, unwilling to accept that God is merciful to *all* who call upon Him; and yet he saw *God* as the problem.

We, too, can get to fussing at God over things that haven't gone our way. It is the height of arrogance to fuss with an omnipotent, infinite, omniscient God who has already extended to us more mercy than we could ever begin to deserve. But all too often, we get wrapped up in our idea of how things should be and become restless within the bounds of God's will.

It is then that the Holy Spirit echoes the words spoken to Jonah *"Doest thou well to be angry for the gourd?"* (Jonah 4:9) Whatever it is we are feeling restless and irritated about, God asks us, *"Doest thou well to be angry?"* Until we confess our arrogance, our pride, our dissatisfaction with the will of God, we can never have the peace which ought to characterize our lives.

What are you tempted to fuss at God about today?

12

God's Blessed Will

"Into Thy blessed will to abide,
Jesus, I come to Thee."

The will of God is something that is spoken of often in Christian circles. Although we may spend lots of time thinking about what God's will for us is, or how we can do God's will, we rarely stop to contemplate what a blessing God's will really is.

Romans 12:2 says that the will of God is *"good, and acceptable, and perfect."* Imagine what life would be like if God's will did not match up to just one of those qualities.

If God's will were not good, life would be a hopeless string of torments. Oh, how terrifying to be trapped in the clutches of an all-powerful being with a malicious heart!

Or if God's will were not acceptable, think of the hopelessness of a universe ruled by a well-meaning being, but whose ability or intellect could not accomplish his desired end.

If God's will were not perfect, we would be thrown upon the whims of a being not *quite* able or willing to make everything come out the way he wants. How grateful I am that God's will is good, acceptable, *and* perfect!

Sometimes, we can fall into the trap of being afraid of God's will. Satan would like nothing more than to see us dragging our feet in unbelief or running away from the will of God in outright rebellion. That's why he so often whispers lies to us about the character of God and His will for us.

For a long time, I thought that if I surrendered to the will of God in the area of singleness, I would be forever miserable, bleak, and desolate. But that wasn't true. That was one of Satan's lies.

How do I know that? Because I did eventually surrender that part of my life to God's will, and once I accepted singleness as part of God's good, acceptable, and perfect design for this season of my life, I was able to rest in His will and be at peace with His plan.

While I resisted His will, singleness seemed purposeless and unfulfilling; but once I yielded to it, He used my singleness to give me a sense of purpose and fulfilment that I never would have experienced had I been given my own will instead.

Truly, God's will *is* a blessed thing when we choose to abide in it!

What part of God's will is the Holy Spirit calling you to abide in today?

13

Out of Myself

"Out of myself to dwell in Thy love"

The book of Jude was written as a warning. False teachers were on the rise among the Christian churches; and Jude wrote to warn them, reminding them of the judgement of God. He describes the false teachers in all their wicked pride and ungodliness; and then, at the end, has this to say to his beloved fellow Christians:

"But ye, beloved, building up yourselves on your most holy faith, praying in the Holy Ghost, Keep yourselves in the love of God, looking for the mercy of our Lord Jesus Christ unto eternal life." (Jude 20-21)

To keep themselves from falling for the self-focus of the false teachers, whose doctrine can be well summarized by the phrase of our day, "Do what makes you happy," Jude gives several admonitions.

Christians who would be strong against Satan's lies must first build themselves upon their *"most holy faith:"* that is, to exercise their faith so that it would grow stronger day by day. They must also pray. I cannot begin to do justice to the importance of a daily, constant communion with God, telling Him all our troubles, thanking Him for His blessings, and listening to what the Holy Spirit wants to communicate to us. These are the foundations which make the next item possible:

> *"Keep yourselves in the love of God."*

That word *keep* literally means to watch or guard. Christians who want to ward off the lies of Satan and combat false doctrine must be careful to guard the love of God in their hearts. It is not love of *self* (which is what the false teachers in Jude's time and our own teach), but love of *God* that motivates us. As Paul says in 2 Corinthians, *"the love of Christ constraineth us" (5:14)* Everything we say, everything we do should flow from the love of God.

But in order to keep or guard the love of God in our lives, we must take our focus off of ourselves and fasten it upon God. As Jude goes on to say,

> *"looking for the mercy of our Lord Jesus Christ unto eternal life."*

We know how deep the love of God is for us because we know what it prompted Jesus to do on our behalf. If we are so deeply loved, how can we keep that to ourselves? We cannot. That is why Jude continues by saying,

> *"And of some have compassion, making a difference: And others save with fear, pulling them out of the fire; hating even the garment spotted by the flesh." (22-23)*

What is God's love motivating you to do today?

14

Raptures Above

"Out of despair into raptures above"

Imagine the despair of entering eternity to find that hell is real, and that you have refused Christ's forgiveness for the last time. The torments, the pain, the terror, all will be real and acute; but perhaps the most horrible part of all will be the utter despair at the fact that there is no hope. You can never escape, you can do nothing to lessen the torments, and there can never be an end to your misery.

Contrast that with the joy of Romans 5: *"Therefore being justified by faith, we have peace with God through our Lord Jesus Christ: By whom also we have access by faith into this grace wherein we stand, and rejoice in hope of the glory of God." (1-2)*

Outside of Christ, eternity holds unending despair; but for the saved in Christ, eternity holds only joy and hope and the unending glory of God. Peace with God, access to His grace, and hope of future glories: all these were bought by Christ's sacrifice.

Just as the horrors of hell will be forever, so the joys of heaven will also be unending. The rapturous rejoicing of the saved in Christ will continue throughout all eternity. As Paul says in Romans 8:18,

> *"For I reckon that the sufferings of this present time are not worthy to be compared with the glory which shall be revealed in us."*

No earthly sorrow can drown out the joy of heaven. On our darkest day, when all earthly joys have crumbled and faded away, heaven will still be unfailingly promised; and our greatest rejoicing will still be ahead of us. The joy of the Christian is not just for a someday in heaven, though. Our eternal joy begins now, as we choose to look with joy towards the city *"whose builder and maker is God". (Hebrews 11:10)*

How will the joy of heaven affect your life today?

15

Upward

"Upward for aye on wings like a dove,
Jesus, I come to Thee"

The term "for aye" is one we don't hear much nowadays. It basically means "forever", or "continually". The joy towards which the hymnist is looking is not just a one-time event. It is to be a continual joy.

The Christian does not look forward to eternity as one might look forward to Christmas, or a vacation, or any other event in life. We look forward to life forever with God, where the night never comes, the day never ends, the joy never fades. In heaven, the light of God's presence will be undiminished, no matter how long we enjoy it for.

But until then, we enjoy just a foretaste, longing for the day when faith shall turn to sight, when we shall no longer see *"through a glass, darkly." (1 Cor. 13:12)* Then, our earthly striving will be ended, once and for all. The psalmist captured the cry of our weary, world-worn hearts when he wrote, *"Oh, that I had wings like a dove! For then would I fly away, and be at rest." (55:6)*

We long for the day, and rejoice that it will come, when *"we shall be like Him; for we shall see Him as He is." (1 John 3:2)* But what is all our longing, our looking forward, our expectant hope, to accomplish? John tells us:

> *"And every man that hath this hope in him purifieth himself, even as He is pure." (1 John 3:3)*

The certain hope, the expectation of the glories and the joys of heaven should prompt us to purify ourselves, to become more and more like Christ. That is the upward flight of the soul in exile, bound to earth, and yet transcending it, *in* the world, but not *of* it.

And so we wait: not passively, but actively, seeking to do the glorious will of God on earth as it is, and will forever be, done in heaven.

What is the hope of seeing God *"as He is"* someday prompting you to change today?

16

The Fear of the Tomb

*"Out of the fear and dread of the tomb,
Jesus, I come, Jesus, I come"*

Have you ever read *Foxe's Book of Martyrs*? It is a difficult read. Throughout the history of Christianity, followers of Christ have been tortured and killed in numerous ways too horrible to imagine. And yet, there are so many stories of men and women who went to their deaths, even long and agonizing deaths, with peace, and even with joy!

How is this possible? Isn't death a fearful thing, especially such gruesome deaths as the martyrs for Christ have endured over the centuries? Why would someone go to their death with a song of joyful praise on their lips?

Simply because in Christ, death is not an end, but a beginning.

Because of the forgiveness bought by Christ's sacrifice, we can be confident that, once our sins have been forgiven, there is a certain place for us in heaven.

We never need to fear death, for it is simply the event that ushers us into the presence of the Most High God, in whose presence there is fulness of joy, and at whose right hand there are pleasures for evermore. (*Psalm 16:11*)

In a passage dealing with the certainty of the resurrection of the saints in Christ at His coming, Paul gives this bit of triumphant truth:

"*O death, where is thy sting? O grave, where is thy victory? The sting of death is sin; and the strength of sin is the law. But thanks be to God, which giveth us the victory through our Lord Jesus Christ.*" (*1 Corinthians 15:55-56*)

The victory already won by Christ has purchased our place by His side for all eternity. So then, death is nothing to be feared, for it is the beginning of endless joy in the presence of God!

Are you living in the truth of the Christ's victory over death today?

17

Eternal Joy and Light

Into the joy and light of Thy home,
Jesus, I come to Thee"

The light of heaven will be unlike any light we have ever seen before. In Revelation 21, John states that he saw

"the great city, the holy Jerusalem, descending out of heaven from God, having the glory of God: and her light was like unto a stone most precious, even like a jasper stone, clear as crystal" (vv. 10-11). Later in the chapter, light comes up again: *"And the city had not need of the sun, neither of the moon, to shine in it; for the glory of God did lighten it, and the Lamb is the light thereof" (v. 23).*

In Revelation 22, it is said that,

"There shall be no night there; and they need no candle, neither light of the sun; for the Lord God giveth them light" (v. 5).

Heaven will be a place filled with the light of the glory of God Himself. There will be no need for any other kind of light, because like God Himself, His light will be omnipresent and immutable. It will never fade, never end: there will be no night, because God never sleeps. His light will never go out, never be obscured; it will just go on shining in all its strength throughout the happy, beautiful, endless day of eternity.

I John 1:5 tells us that, *"God is light, and in Him is no darkness at all."* Just as the light of heaven reflects the attributes of its Source, we, too, are to be like the moon, reflecting back the light of Another, the light of the glory of God.

Our light should be different from the world's light. It should be purer, brighter, more constant and unwavering. It should be a beacon in the dark world, lighting the way to the land where there is no night.

How does God want you to reflect His light today?

18

Ruin Untold

"Out of the depths of ruin untold"

Jesus told a parable about a rich man, who had enjoyed life to its fullest. There was also a beggar, named Lazarus, who sat at his gate. The rich man lived out his life consumed with his riches, while the beggar possessed nothing but faith in God. We know that Lazarus had faith in God, because both men died, and Lazarus was welcomed into "Abraham's bosom" (heaven.) But the rich man had not believed; and when he died, he was cast into hell.

"And in hell he lift up his eyes, being in torments, and seeth Abraham afar off, and Lazarus in his bosom. And he cried and said, Father Abraham, have mercy on me, and send Lazarus, that he may dip the tip of his finger in water, and cool my tongue; for I am tormented in this flame. But Abraham said, Son, remember that thou in thy lifetime recievedst thy good things, and likewise Lazarus evil things: but now he is comforted, and thou art tormented. And beside all this, between us and you there is a great gulf fixed: so that they which would pass from hence to you cannot; neither can they pass to us, that would come from thence."

You could go on through the rest of the story and read of the rich man's plea for someone to tell his brothers of their impending doom before it is too late, but my point in bringing to your notice this particular part of the parable is that the rich man found himself in a place of utter ruin. Death had stripped him of all his riches, of his every source of comfort, of everything he had valued in life. Worse still, it was too late for mercy. Abraham could not help him, because hell is an everlasting destination.

It is good to stop every once in a while and remember the woeful existence from which we have been rescued. When Christ saved you, He did more than just purchase eternal joy: He saved you from eternal torment.

> *When was the last time you thanked God for saving you from "ruin untold" in hell?*

19

God's Shelter

"Into the peace of Thy sheltering fold"

In Bible times, sheep were often kept in sheepfolds, which were walled stone enclosures with a door or gap in the wall were the sheep would go in and out. The sheepfold was a place of safety and peace for the sheep. Within its walls, they felt secure.

At night, the shepherd would lay in front of the door, guarding his sheep from any thieves or predators that might want to get into the sheepfold. In the morning, it was the shepherd's voice that would call them out to pasture.

In John 10, Jesus not only tells us that He is the good shepherd that *"giveth His life for the sheep."*

He also says, *"I am the door of the sheep. All that ever came before Me are thieves and robbers: but the sheep did not hear them. I am the door: by Me if any man enter in, he shall be saved, and shall go in and out and find pasture."* (John 10:7-9)

Jesus not only guards the door, He *is* the door. Once inside the fold of the saved in Christ, we have the peace and security of knowing that the door is safely guarded: no harm can come to us, for nothing can sneak past the all-seeing Shepherd.

And who are His sheep?

"My sheep hear My voice, and they follow Me: And I give them eternal life; and they shall never perish, neither shall any man pluck them out of my Father's hand. I and My Father are one." (John 10:27-30)

When we trusted Christ for salvation, we were taken out of the anxiety, uncertainty, and fear of the unsaved. We were placed in the sheepfold, there to enjoy peace, rest, and security, knowing that no man can pluck us from the hands that were nail-pierced on our behalf.

The security of the sheepfold can be seen in Romans 8:38-39, where Paul gives the rapturous truth:

"For I am persuaded, that neither death, nor life, nor angels, nor principalities, nor powers, nor things present, nor things to come, Nor height, nor depth, nor any other creature, shall be able to separate us from the love of God, which is in Christ Jesus our Lord."

How does the security of Christ the Door bring peace to your heart today?

20

Ever Beholding

"Ever Thy glorious face to behold"

The joy of eternity for the saved in Christ has many facets, but perhaps the most exquisite expectation of the exiled believer is that of one day seeing God in person.

We long to see the face of Him whom, as Peter said, *"having not seen, ye love; in whom, though now ye see Him not, yet believing, ye rejoice with joy unspeakable and full of glory: Receiving the end of your faith, even the salvation of your souls."(I Peter1:8-9)* It is easier to bear the longing when we are anticipating the joy of the day when we will actually be forever with the Lord.

Of course, whether we live longing for the day to come, or rejoicing that it will someday arrive, is simply dependent upon whether we choose to live in the longing or in the joy. We have access to the joy of certain hope *now*, regardless of the fact that we must wait to see the Lord face-to-face. But I do not think it is wrong to long for the day when the joyful eternity in God's presence will begin.

It's like a small child, knowing that summer will soon begin, and school will be over. He or she may long for the summer, but that longing rarely makes children morose. There is too much excitement about the expected reality of summer for a child to be cast down by the longing that it would come. That is the way we are when we choose to live in the joy of the future, even when we are longing for the future to begin *now*.

David often showcased the perspective of living in the joy to come. In Psalm 17:15 he wrote:

"As for me, I will behold Thy face in righteousness: I shall be satisfied, when I awake, with Thy likeness."

Part of the joy of beholding the face of God is that, when we do, we will become like Him. (1 John 3:3)

In heaven, we will be able to stand before the face of God without the terror of a sinner before a holy God. We will stand there in Christ's righteousness, worshipping Him in the beauty of holiness for all eternity.

With such a glorious future ahead, we have cause to be joyful, no matter what is going on around us. The life we live now in the joy of heaven transcends the cares of this world. Those cares are for a moment; our joy is for all eternity!

> ***Are you living today in the longing of the moment or the joy of the future?***

21

Come

"Jesus, I Come to Thee"

At the end of the very last book of the Bible, John writes these words of invitation:

"And the Spirit and the bride say, Come. And let him that heareth say, Come. And let him that is athirst come. And whosoever will, let him take the water of life freely." (Revelation 22:17)

The joy, peace, hope, redemption, cleansing, shelter, and rest offered by Christ are free. All we have to do is choose to come to Him.

Colossians 2:6-7 says, *"As ye have therefore received Christ Jesus the Lord, so walk ye in Him: Rooted and built up in Him, and stablished in the faith, as ye have been taught, abounding therein with thanksgiving."*

The same way we came to Christ for salvation is the same way we come to Him for everything else: humbly, depending wholly on His grace, desiring for Him to cleanse us and grow us up in Him. But this coming to Him for sanctification must be daily, for we so quickly drift away from Him.

The Christian life is built on Christ, rooted and grown up in Him as we study, memorize, and meditate on the Word of God, and keep ourselves close to Him in constant conversation through prayer. That is how we make the benefits of a temporary reminder like this devotional last.

Your spiritual growth will only continue as long as you are yielded to the Spirit. When we put off the things that make us grow in Christlikeness and make way for the things that feed our flesh, we stunt our growth and grieve the Holy Spirit. Coming to Him daily helps us keep on the track of growth in godliness while deepening our relationship with God.

My prayer for you, dear reader, as you close this book and go on with life is that you will make time to come to God daily, seeking Him wholeheartedly and living in the joy, peace, and hope of His promises. It's not enough just to *come* to Jesus: He wants you to *stay* close to Him.

"I am the vine, ye are the branches: He that abideth in Me, and I in him, the same bringeth forth much fruit: for without Me ye can do nothing."

John 15:5

www.ingramcontent.com/pod-product-compliance
Lightning Source LLC
Chambersburg PA
CBHW071037080526
44587CB00015B/2664